Controlling Your Money

The Battle to Save Our Future

By
Edward F Gray

DISCLAIMER:

The information provided in this book is for informational purposes only and is not intended to be a source of advice regarding the material presented. The information and examples in this book do not constitute legal or financial advice. Consult with a financial professional to determine what may be best for your individual needs.

The publisher and the author make no guarantee or other promise as to any results that may be obtained from using the content of this book. You should never make any investment decision without first consulting with your own financial advisor and conducting your own research and due diligence. To the maximum extent permitted by law, the publisher and the author disclaim any and all liability if any information, commentary, analysis, opinions, advice and/or recommendations contained in this book prove inaccurate, incomplete or unreliable, or result in any investment or other losses.

Content contained and provided in this book is not intended to and does not constitute legal advice or investment advice. The publisher and the author are providing this book and its contents on an "as is" basis. Use of the information in this book is at your own risk.

Acknowledgements

To JJ, Bryce and Kennedy, through this book, my hope is that I have found the words to assist you on understanding what will become yours to control and direct.

To my good friends Jay and Joe, without you and our many discussions on money and finances, I would not have found my voice and the courage to put it out there. Thank you.

To my Mother, you have always been my biggest supporter. You have shown me that once you decide you want something in life, nothing denies unwavering faith.

To my late Father, you bestowed upon me one of my greatest strengths, to question everything and keep asking why until you find the truth for yourself.

To Amed, thank you for your mentorship, wisdom and guidance. Your imprint on my mindset is on display daily. Thank you, my brother.

To Robert, thank you for the discussions on money and mindset. You hammer that home for many daily. Thank you.

To Sandy, Thoreau would struggle with the words to describe how grateful I am that we share a life together. Through ups and downs, your patience and compassion have shone bright. I am blessed to share a life with you.

I must stress to you, be patient and kind to yourself. Allow yourself the time to fully digest the concept and its many benefits. Once you finish the book, if you believe this concept would work in your life, then start the research and self-education process. I also warn you, there is much misinformation on the concept. I've added a resource section in the back of the book to assist you. It is imperative that to fully grasp the concept, you go to the source and those who honor the source's mission for your research and education.

Good luck on your financial journey.

Ed

Contents

money and the human need for safety become a struggle, our stress levels increase dramatically.

In a recent survey by the Thriving Wallet on money and stress, there were 5 key findings I want to highlight.

90% of individuals say that money affects their stress level
Above 65% report feeling that their financial difficulties are piling up so much they can't overcome them
40% report they are taking no notable steps to secure their financial future
40% wish they could have a fresh financial start
25% make purchases they later regret when experiencing financial stress

So, what are we stressing about? Here are the top 5.

Retirement – 51%
Buying a home – 51%
Purchasing/leasing a car – 44%
Daily leisure activities – 36%
Purchasing clothes/groceries – 34%

The survey findings and the top stressors all involve the human need for safety and varying levels of emotions.

Money Mindset

Money mindsets are programs that run on autopilot. They are our own set of unique experiences with money. Often, they are developed when we were young. They can be opinions from our parents, family, friends, coworkers, teachers and the content we consume (especially marketing).

Once you have a fully developed money mindset, it becomes the lens you make decisions from. A person's money mindset could be great if they grew up around people with an abundance mindset or it could be very limiting if it was the opposite (scarcity).

Below are often repeated statements that impact our money mindset.

- Money doesn't grow on trees
- Money is the root of all evil
- The rich get rich and the poor get poorer
- I'm not good with money
- Money can't buy happiness

How many of these have you heard?

How many have your parents said to you?

How many have your friends or peers said in your presence?

How many have you ever said?

None of us have the same money mindset. Each person's life experiences, environment and beliefs are unique to them. The concept and the vehicle used to implement it, are often generalized and critiqued by well-respected financial gurus, bloggers, and advisors. We must do our homework. The truth can't be bent if facts are available. The concept benefits are facts that can't be questioned (I will detail why in coming chapters).

A person with a limiting money mindset will struggle when we go over the concept. Overcoming a limiting money mindset can be done but, not without adding the key elements below.

- An open and curious mind
- Desire to find the truth
- Keep asking why

- Letting go of being wrong
- Deprogramming yourself (affirmations and/or subconscious reprogramming)

What's Next?

We will now go over the concept and the vehicle that runs it most efficiently. If you run into any resistance within, come back to the Money Mindset section and read the key elements necessary to overcoming a limiting money mindset again.

2
The Concept and The Vehicle

If I told you a rock-solid plan existed for using your money in a way that would change your life, the life of your family and generations to come, would you be excited?

"Hell Yeah"

That was my response when I first was asked that question in 2016. But alas, I fell victim to the limiting money mindset and didn't officially start until early 2019.

The Concept

The concept is called IBC. IBC stands for the Infinite Banking Concept. The idea came to the late R Nelson Nash after much reflection, critical thinking and prayer in the early 1980s. He spent the better part of the next 35 years traveling and teaching the concept to the public.

So, what is IBC really? It is a method of managing capital (your money) via a private contract between you and a participating mutual life insurance company. It must be a participating mutual life insurance company. A participating mutual life insurance company entitles the owners of a whole life insurance policy, the right to share in the earnings surplus. From here on out when I mention mutual life insurance company know that I am referring to a participating one. The private contract is a whole life insurance policy. The power lies in the specific use, structure, and design of the whole life insurance policy contract. It is imperative you contract with a mutual life insurance company and not a public/private insurance company. Choosing the public/private option will negate ownership benefits you enjoy when contracting with a mutual insurance company.

I will stop right here because the elephant in the room must be addressed. Stick with me here, R Nelson Nash did Noble Prize-worthy research that was divinely inspired. He came up with IBC as the most efficient place to store your capital and use it. The vehicle that runs the concept most efficiently is whole life insurance through a mutual life insurance company. I also remind you I am not an insurance agent but an owner of multiple IBC policies. I'm not selling you an insurance policy. I'm sharing with you a better way to live financially.

The Noise

- Whole life insurance is outrageously expensive
- Insurance companies keep your cash value when you die
- The average rate of return on whole life insurance is not as good as the stock market average
- Why would anyone pay interest to borrow their own money?
- It is great for rich people and the agents that sell it

1) Whole life insurance is outrageously expensive. Expensive is relative to an individual's perspective. This is also a generic statement. The open-minded and curious person would be asking questions.

    - What value do I receive for buying whole life insurance?
    - Is there a direct relationship between how much I pay in and the value I receive in return?
    - Expensive compared to what?

Question 1

Is there any way possible that a whole life insurance policy could be structured that would be beneficial to a person's financial life from the start of a policy?

The answer you receive to that question will separate real knowledge from uneducated opinion or limiting money mindset.

Question 2

If whole life insurance is as bad as you say it is, could you explain why banks have billions of dollars in these policies?

Most people won't know this, but again the level of detail in their answers will reveal insight into their knowledge.

IBC – Proper Structure of a Whole Life Insurance Policy

(Disclaimer: Again, I remind you I am not a licensed insurance agent. What I will share with you is my personal experience in setting up my policies for educational purposes. Trust but verify always!)

I will try to make this simple and not get too in the weeds.

A whole life insurance policy has two components you want to be aware of and understand.

Whole Life Insurance Policy Structure (Vanilla)

The vanilla whole life insurance policy has two components.

Base Premium (Death Benefit)

The base premium is directly correlated to your death benefit. The higher the death benefit, the higher the base premium. Now many factors play into the cost, which I will not go into in detail. They are age, health, lab work results, and all the questions you answer when filling out a life insurance application.

Cash Value

Eventually a part of the base premium you pay, will make its way into the cash value side of your whole life insurance policy. It varies by company but it takes years to build up. Remember, this is how a vanilla policy would work. I will not go into details because it is not ideal for practicing IBC.

Whole Life Insurance Policy Structure (IBC)

There are some differing perspectives within the IBC community (insurance agents) on how to set up a properly structured IBC policy. The differing perspectives are around the % of base premium in relation to the % of cash value. I myself have concluded this depends on how the customer is planning on using their IBC policy, their financial goals and their comfort level in required premium. There certainly could be other reasons but it really comes down to customer preference and having a thorough discussion with an IBC knowledgeable insurance agent. It is a process that must be approached with educational responsibility and relationship building.

Base Premium (IBC Policy)

There is no difference on how the base premium works from an insurance standpoint. The difference is in the

% of overall premium paid in relationship to the rider we will be discussing next.

PUA (Paid-Up Additional) Rider

We will reference the paid-up additional rider as PUA Rider from here on out (some insurance companies have other names for them, but they are all cash riders). The PUA Rider is the rocket fuel in the engine of the IBC. When you add a PUA Rider to your whole life insurance policy, it gives you the contractual right to add cash directly into your policy's cash value.

Base Premium & PUA Design

Optimal design on an IBC policy will fall somewhere between these two examples.

1) 10% to 50% Base Premium

2) 50% to 90% PUA Rider

My First IBC Policy

Overall Premium: $8K

Base Premium: $2K (25%)

PUA Rider: $6K (75%)

In the next chapter, I am going to lay out the individual benefits of a properly structured whole life insurance policy designed to practice IBC. It will be straightforward and high level.

3
IBC Policy Owner Benefits

We have learned that the PUA Rider is the rocket fuel in the engine that runs IBC. Now we will look at the benefits enjoyed by the owner of a properly structured IBC Policy.

The benefits we will list out have an overarching theme that connects them together to benefit the policy owner. That theme is financial control in a very favorable environment.

7 IBC Policy Owner Benefits

- Safety: The owner's money suffers no losses
- Liquidity: The owner's money is available to them in less than a week and with minimal paperwork
- Guaranteed Growth: The owner's money multiplies
- Leverage: The owner can use their money as collateral
- Flexibility: The owner has flexibility in funding, access and terms
- Protections: The owner has multiple protections: Inflation Hedge, Private, Regulatory, Fees and Death Benefit
- Tax Advantaged: An owner receives both tax-free growth and tax-free access

Safety

Is your money safe? Over the past 100 years, there have been two financial recessions/depressions that affected many people. The great depression of 1929 and the 2008 great financial recession. During both trying times in our country, thousands of banks went bankrupt. Not one mutual life insurance company went under during those two major financial events. If a mutual life insurance company were to go under, it would not affect the safety of your money. Each state has provisions in place that allow other mutual life insurance companies to step in and take on all the insolvent insurance companies contracts. Does that feel like a safe place to store your capital?

Liquidity

The cash value side of your whole life insurance policy is a contract between you and the insurance company. As a policy owner, you are contractually, a part-owner of the company per your premiums paid in. This is spelled out in the contract and owners are listed first for who can borrow against the cash value of their policy. During times of tightening credit, you will not have to worry one bit. Going back to our safety example, many people during the great depression of 1929 used their cash value in their whole life insurance policies to keep their businesses afloat and provide for their families. Really makes you think did anyone in the Thriving Wallet survey have whole life insurance. And if they did, we can bet their level of financial stress was minimized.

Guaranteed Growth

The growth in your policy will come from two places. The first is the guaranteed growth of your cash value (4%). Some companies have lower guaranteed growth (3%). The guaranteed growth rate is not as significant as it may seem once we see what happens to dividends once they are received. The second is the base premium is eligible for dividends each year. During the beginning of a whole life policy, the dividends you receive will be minimal.

However, each year it will increase. Another powerful concept often missed is that once a dividend is declared and paid by an insurance company, it becomes a part of the cash value side of your policy. This means that the previous year's dividend is now contractually guaranteed to grow at 4% until you die. As we have stated throughout this book a whole life insurance policy with a mutual insurance company is a private contract with a contractually guaranteed growth rate on your cash value of 4%. To add even more peace of mind is that if a massive financial collapse occurs, a mutual insurance company cannot go bankrupt. Each state has provisions for other mutual insurance companies to assume the contracts as we outlined in the safety benefit. This solidifies the guarantee for the growth of the cash value.

Leverage

Only one financial product in existence allows you to leverage cash as collateral, while also contractually guaranteeing your cash will grow uninterrupted at 4%. That product is whole life insurance.

A loan taken against your cash value, can be done online and in less than 3 minutes. There are other ways of leveraging assets, but none are as quick, efficient and have the flexibility benefits we will go over next.

Flexibility

The flexibility of a whole life insurance policy is a very attractive benefit for when life happens. You can fund the policies however you want (monthly, quarterly, semi-annually, yearly). You deposit cash through the PUA Rider, whenever you want and as often as you want throughout the year. You can carry over unused PUA limits to the next year if you want. There are no restrictions on how many loans you can have and how you pay the loans back. You control when and how much you pay back to the loans.

Anytime you want a loan, you can do it online and have the cash in 3 days or so with very minimal paperwork. Now some companies are more flexible than others, so you will want to do your due diligence and ask questions. But even the least flexible mutual insurance company is better than any other industry's financial vehicles when it comes to flexibility.

Protections

There are few products out there that will beat the real rate of inflation. Whole life insurance is one of those products. When you combine the guaranteed growth rate of 4% and the dividend (1-2%) you have a solid vehicle that will stay ahead of inflation. Very important to remember are the two tailwinds that allow this to happen: taxes and fees. There are no taxes or fees on the growth of your cash value and dividends. Commonly you will hear that dividends are not guaranteed and that is a true statement. However, what is also true is that no mutual insurance company over the last 100 years has failed to pay a dividend. So, history is on your side.

Life insurance is private contract between you (the owner of the policy) and the insurance company. It doesn't show up on a credit report and there is no requirement to report it on a tax return (provided you keep it in force and use it efficiently). You also receive creditor protection benefits (scope varies by state/law).

Life insurance has been around before the US income tax code was created in 1913. They are private contracts and free from most government regulation. There has been only one time that the IRS stepped in to stop what was going on in the life insurance industry.

That time was in the 1980s. This is where the regulatory term MEC (Modified Endowment Contract) limit originated from. It is also why we can only put in 9 times the base premium into cash. The IRS ruled that if you buy life insurance with a death benefit premium of say $100 you can't then add a PUA Rider on it and put in $25 million dollars.

There were rich people buying life insurance with a very minimal amount of death benefit and setting up PUA Riders that allowed them to add in millions of dollars. Remember what we know about life insurance, it is tax-free. The IRS was not going to let that continue to happen. We still have a wonderful product to practice IBC with even with the MEC limitation.

While there are fees for the PUA Rider they are one-time fees. There are no fees on accessing the cash value of your policy via loans. Yes, there are interest rates on the loans you take against your cash value but there are three very big factors working for you when you borrow against your cash value.

1) Cash value does not stop growing at 4% guaranteed.

2) A dividend is still paid on your cash value and base premium.

3) Loan rates are such that you are borrowing at close to a net interest rate of 0%, when you factor in the guaranteed growth and the dividend.

Last, we have what life insurance was created for, the death benefit. The death benefit protects your human life value. If you die suddenly, your beneficiaries receive a tax-free death benefit, at a time of sorrow and when no one wants to worry about going to work or doing much of anything.

Tax Advantaged

Whole life insurance has been called the rich man's Roth IRA. While that is true, it is also a limiting money mindset. Whole life insurance is a wonderful tax-free growth vehicle for anyone. Sure, you need to put money into it but, wouldn't you rather put money into a vehicle you own and have full control over? Think about it. The power of tax-free growth is huge and that is why many people love the Roth IRA/Roth 401K. What most are missing is how powerful tax-free growth is when you combine it with guaranteed 4% growth and uninterrupted compounding until the day you die.

Tax-free distribution is another powerful advantage to the policy owner. How we access cash when the time arrives for passive income is a shift in the money mindset. Remember the cash value of the policy is yours to use as you want (full control). Sure, you could take the dividends and have them come right to you but, why do that and stop the power of compounding on those dividends. Policy loans are not income to the IRS. What is income to the IRS is taking out more money then you put into a life insurance contract.

Remember, the IRS is looking at life insurance through the lens of the death benefit. We don't have to do that. Loans are not income to the IRS, but they are income to you if that is what you decide to do. The reason this works lies in the power of uninterrupted compound interest. When passive income time arrives, all policy owners have the right to take loans out each year against their cash value and never pay them back. The key is you can only take a loan in an amount fully covered by your cash value's growth.

4
IBC Strategies

IBC can be used in any number of financially creative ways and you're only limited by your imagination. I want to give you food for thought and some ideas to apply to your own financial life. Financial efficiency and using our capital, while also building it, can assist in making tremendous progress in our financial lives.

There are 3 key areas that many IBC policy owners use their cash value for, to improve their financial lives. We will go into detail on each one and provide real world scenarios.

1) Debt Elimination

2) Ongoing Life Expenses

3) Investment & Business

Debt Elimination

The average non-mortgage debt per US household is somewhere between $25K to $30K, depending on which survey source you check. What is silently destroying the wealth of many Americans is a fundamental misunderstanding of interest and how it is applied.

The Volume of Interest

I want you to picture yourself at a car dealership. You have picked out the car you want, it is within your budget and now you are ready to sign and drive. You secured financing for 48 months at 4.99% for a 2015 Ford Focus.

Here are the terms you signed your name to:

Financing Amount: $15K
Interest Rate: 4.99%
Term Length: 48
Monthly Payment: $345.37

This seems like it is not a bad deal at all. It is 2020 and the average cost of a new car is $36K or so. You were frugal and spent less than half of that.

Math never lies but it can most certainly mislead. I will add one extra figure to the financing terms above and reveal the bait and switch that goes on every day in the world of finance.

Financing Amount: $15K
Interest Rate: 4.99%
Volume of Interest: 18% (1st month's interest charge: $62.37 / $345.37)
Term Length: 48
Monthly Payment: $345.37

No matter how you calculate the numbers, your first month's payment of $345.37 for your 2015 Ford Focus is putting $62.37 into the pocket of the lender. This is true of every type of loan you will find out there. Some are worse than others, but it is the volume of interest that is a silent destroyer of wealth.

A Better Way – The IBC Way

Now let's say you walk onto the same car lot and there is the 2015 Ford Focus that fits your budget. The only difference is now you don't need to go into the financing guys office at the dealership because you have an IBC policy with $15K of available cash value.

Now the conversation you have with the car salesman about purchasing the vehicle will put the power of negotiation on your side. He who has the gold (cash) makes the rules. There is always a cash price that is lower than a financing price on car lots.

The IBC Car Loan Numbers

Ok to drill this home I need you to take a deep breath and get ready to go into the weeds. We need to do this to fully grasp how much financing a car purchase using your IBC policy improves your financial efficiency and builds your capital.

IBC Cash Value: $20K
Policy Loan: $15K
Interest Rate: 6%
Term Length: Owner Discretion
Monthly Payment: Owner Discretion

IBC Flexibility Benefit

First, let's address "Owner Discretion". Do you remember in the previous chapter we went over the 7 IBC Policy Owner Benefits? The benefit of flexibility grants the policy owner the choice to pay a policy loan back in whatever way works best for the policy owner. Now it is best to capitalize your IBC policy and pay your loans back. But, if you have a tough month financially or lose your job, you have the right to exercise the option not to pay the loan back.

IBC Guaranteed Growth & Leverage Benefit

The synergy between guaranteed growth and leverage in an IBC policy is where we see how much better it is for us financially to control our money in a vehicle that benefits the policy owner first. Now we will run the numbers.

IBC Cash Value: \$20K
Policy Loan: \$15K
Interest Rate: 6%
First Year Interest Cost: \$900
First Year Guaranteed Growth: \$800
First Year Dividend (1.5%): \$300

What jumps out to you from the numbers above?

Math doesn't lie.

\$1100 > \$800 am I right?

You might be thinking. So, am I being paid to buy a car?

You could look at it that way, but that would be shortchanging the opportunity before you. The interest that insurance companies charge is simple interest. In short, that means the interest doesn't compound upon itself.

Why does that matter?

The cash value growth in your policy compounds and gives you an advantage on the growth side vs the interest expense side. The loan payment you make to the insurance company, for the car you just bought will have a credit of interest back to you.

Let's look at the numbers.

You decide to make a monthly payment of $350 to the $15K loan balance. All $350 will be applied to the total amount of $15K and $800 (1-year simple interest). Your balance will be something like the following:

Old Loan Balance: $15800
Loan Payment: $350
Interest Credit: $21.15
Loan Balance After Payment: $15428.85

You will see an interest credited back to you on every loan payment. This is powerful.

Below is a payment I made to a policy loan on my IBC policy in late 2019. Notice the interest credited back.

Notice Date: 12/02/2019

AUL Individual Customer Service
Telephone Number: 1-800-537-6442

Thank You

For Your Loan Payment

Old Loan Balance	$ 5,127.04
Amount Applied Effective 12/02/2019	$ 350.00
Prepaid Interest Refund Applied To Principal	$ 7.98
Loan Balance After Payment	$ 4,769.06

Loan Interest Rate 4.760%
Policy Loan Interest Paid To: 05/22/2020

A very important distinction not to overlook on the capital building side, is that due to this loan payment, my cash value available increased by $357.98. The interest credited back to me becomes immediately available to use again if needed.

IBC Benefits VS Paying Cash

There are many people out there that swear by paying cash for everything. We will go over the opportunity cost of paying with cash and how it is destroying the wealth of anyone who decides that paying cash is financially savvy.

Tim and Terry are good friends, but they have very different money mindsets with debt. Tim pays cash for everything. Terry practices IBC and understands the value of leveraging his capital, preserving it and having it grow. They both know they need new cars. Tim uses cash and Terry leverages his IBC policy via a loan. They both purchase cars that cost $10K

The Cash Scenario

Tim has savings of $10K and uses it all to buy his car. He now has $0 in savings, but he is happy as he also has no car payment. Tim also knows his last car lasted him about 4 years so he will need to save $2500 a year to be ready to buy his next car with cash.

Tim's Numbers

Tim starts saving $2500 a year in his high yield savings account earning 1.5%

Year 1 Tim has $2537.50 in his savings
Year 2 Tim has $5113.06 in his savings
Year 3 Tim has $7727.25 in his savings
Year 4 Tim has $10380.66 in his savings

The IBC Scenario

Terry set up his IBC policy last year and he has $10K available in the cash value of his policy. He takes out a loan (leverage) against his cash value (collateral) to buy his car.

Terry's Numbers

Terry is earning a contractually guaranteed 4% on his $9500. We must account for the 5% rider fee the insurance company charges for a PUA deposit.

Year 1 Terry has $9880 in his cash value
Year 2 Terry has $10275.20 in his cash value
Year 3 Terry has $10686.20 in his cash value
Year 4 Terry has $11113.65 in his cash value

We also can't forget Terry will earn dividends each year. We will say Terry earns a modest 1% dividend each year (it is very likely it will be higher).

Year 1 Terry earned a $95 dividend
Year 2 Terry earned a $102.75 dividend
Year 3 Terry earned a $106.86 dividend
Year 4 Terry earned a $111.13 dividend

All told Terry earned $1113.65 in interest and dividends of $415.74 for $1529.39.

But Wait It Gets Better!

It is often overlooked but it is a true statement. "A dividend paid goes straight to the cash value and becomes part of the cash value. Therefore, it becomes a part of the overall cash value, upon which the contractually guaranteed 4% is paid." Let's run the numbers again with this information.

Year 1 Terry has $9880 cash value + $98.80 dividend = $9978.80
Year 2 Terry has $10377.95 cash value + $103.78 dividend = $10481.75
Year 3 Terry has $10901.00 cash value + $109.01 dividend = $11010.01
Year 4 Terry has $11450.41 cash value + $114.50 dividend = $11564.92

Now, Terry has $1638.82 in interest and dividends of $426.09 for a total of $2064.91.

What about the loan interest?

We can't ignore the cost of capital, so to keep it an apples to apples comparison, we will say Terry paid a 5% loan interest rate and paid back the loan in 4 years. Terry pays $1054.11 in interest to the insurance company.

The Final Numbers

Tim made $380.66 in interest over the 4 years he saved up for his next car.

Terry made $1010.80 in interest over the 4 years he paid his loan/interest because his cash value continued to earn uninterrupted compound interest inside his IBC policy.

But wait, someone owes taxes in this comparison. Who do you think it is?

Poor Tim owes taxes on his $380.66. Tim must pay out $76.04 (20%) in taxes bringing his total interest earned to $303.62 now. Terry does not owe taxes because of the tax-advantaged status of IBC policy owners.

Total Interest Earned (4 years)

Terry: $1010.80
Tim: $303.62

If we ran this again for Tim and Terry buying another car, the spread between what Terry is earning would grow even higher because of the power of uninterrupted compound growth.

Ongoing Life Expenses

There is plenty of opportunity to redirect money used for ongoing expenses in our lives. There are two types of ongoing expenses. The expected expenses and the unknown expenses. The expected expenses we will go over are not the monthly ones we all have, but they are the ones that are billed quarterly, semi-annually and annually.

These include many of the following:

1) Vehicle Insurance & Maintenance
2) Taxes
3) Utility Bills
4) Subscriptions, Association Fees, etc.

The unknown expenses are ones that we don't know when they will occur or what amount they may cost us. At best we are taking a guess of how much and when.

These include many of the following:

1) Vehicle Repairs
2) Home Repairs
3) Unexpected Travel (Death, Sickness, Weddings, Showers, etc.)

There are over seven but many of these touch us all at some point over a given year.

The IBC Opportunity

Are you budgeting for any of the expenses we talked about in the previous section?

If you answered yes, then where are you storing the money?

Most folks are storing the money in a checking account or savings account. I was doing the same thing a little over a year ago. Now having a budget and planning for future expenses is a step in the right direction.

But is it the most efficient way to store our money?

We know the answer is a resounding NO!

There is opportunity for us in the existing cash flow we have right now! When I started the conversation in my head with how I would come up with $8K to $12K for an IBC policy, I ran smack into my money mindset.

Limited Money Mindset

How are you going to come up with that much money, we don't have it!

I stopped myself and thought that is a limiting way to think. I decided to write it down and reframe it as a better question. This is what I came up with and I know you can use it too.

Unlimited Money Mindset

Are there ways you are using money now, that you could change and find the money to fund an IBC policy?

By reframing the question, I found what I call stagnant money. This is money just sitting in a high yield savings account, waiting for something to happen.

The two biggest chunks of money I found were in my budget for unknown expenses. The other two were in the expected expenses.

Here they are below with the amounts.

1) $5K - Household/Vehicle Expense Savings
2) $1.2K – Vehicle Insurance
3) $1K – Vehicle Maintenance & Registration
4) $1K – Travel Expense Savings

Just those four expenses allowed me to improve my financial efficiency by starting an IBC policy with money I did not need immediately. This is just four I found quickly. There were smaller ones that I'll list below that opened my eyes and improved my money mindset.

1) Annual Subscriptions (Amazon, Dropbox, AAA, Spotify)
2) Sewer/Water
3) Trash
4) HOA

Do any of these expenses show up in your life?

These and any others you may have that I've not listed are your opportunity to use your money more efficiently. It comes down to becoming a financial investigator of how our money flows and where it goes. If you can redirect money to flow to you before going somewhere else, you are doing what the wonderful book "The Richest Man in Babylon" is all about.

"Pay yourself first."

Now let's really supercharge it. I got so amped up when this hit me. I was paying myself first by keeping the money for expenses in my savings account.

How many benefits did I receive for paying myself first in my savings account?

1) Safety
2) Liquidity
3) Control

That is about it. There is growth but it is not guaranteed. I have some protection, no leverage and minimal flexibility. There are no tax advantages to saving money in a savings account.

Now I had been consuming so much content about the IBC strategy I was waking up during the night thinking about it. I even dreamt about it. One day while I was taking a walk at work. A voice spoke up inside of me and said:

"You can get paid to pay your bills."

Now that sounds silly, right? Almost silly enough to be a late-night infomercial!

But I sat with that statement for a while and thought about it. It was true. It was better than I first thought when it first crossed my mind. I can get paid to pay a bill but not just once. I can get paid every year until the day I die.

Turning a $1K Bill Into $93,885,21

As of the writing of this book, I am 48 years young. I decided not to store the thousand dollars I set aside each year for vehicle maintenance and registration in a savings account. Instead, I'm sending it to the PUA Rider of my IBC policy. It will grow to $93,885.21 after 40 years. I'm keeping it simple here and not adding in dividends, just the 4% guaranteed uninterrupted growth that my policy will contractually pay every year.

How is this possible you ask?

1) Every year send $1000 to PUA Rider (Net $950)
2) Compounds uninterrupted every year at 4% for 40 years

How about if you only do it once?

How much would you have for just redirecting a bill of $1K just once and leaving it to accrue at 4% guaranteed uninterrupted growth for 40 years?

The answer is $4,560.97.

The biggest takeaway is the devasting effects of opportunity cost. We are killing the growth of our money by paying cash to someone else before we pay ourselves first.

It is a shift in the money mindset. Send the money to your IBC policy first and everything will start working to your advantage financially. It won't seem like much initially but keep doing it for 5 or 6 years and it adds up.

What Option Sounds Best for You Financially?

Option 1

You put a thousand dollars into a savings account and then take it out to use it to pay a bill. Now that thousand dollars is gone forever and will never earn for you again.

Option 2

You put a thousand dollars into the PUA rider of your IBC policy. You now have $950 available to you quickly and for every year until the day you die it will grow tax-free at 4% guaranteed growth without interruption. You can leverage it and use it as many times as you want during your life.

We all have stagnant money somewhere in our financial lives. The quicker you can find it and use it more efficiently, the quicker you can improve your financial life.

Investment & IBC

This section may or may not apply to you. If you don't invest or you're not interested in investing at all, that is ok. You can dramatically improve your financial life just by using IBC for debt elimination and ongoing expenses.
Now, if you do have an interest in investing or you own a business, then this is another wonderful opportunity to utilize an IBC policy to improve your financial life.

The Arbitrage Opportunity

Arbitrage is the practice of taking advantage of a price difference between two financial vehicles.

Years ago, in the mid-1990s, I worked at a bank called MBNA. I saw firsthand how one person used arbitrage and it has stuck with me ever since. My job involved processing balance transfers in the bank's credit card division. One afternoon I was processing a very large balance transfer for a cardholder into his checking account. I transferred $100K at 0% for 15 months without a transaction fee. You can't do this now, as all banks now charge a transfer fee, but in the mid-1990s, you could.

The gentleman I processed the balance transfer for, was very chatty (we will call him Bill). Bill told me he was going to buy a 1-year CD at 5% from his local bank and at the end of the term, he would have $5K in interest. Bill would then pay back his MBNA credit card and pocket the $5K for himself (he did have to pay taxes on the $5K).

Bill told me he planned on calling back MBNA and asking what 0% offers they had available for him. The rinse and repeat method. I saw opportunity and asked Bill if I could just call him directly and handle his transfer for him in a year. He agreed and we did transfers of $100K two more times before the party ended (no more free transactions).

It didn't hit me until years later while reading about Warren Buffet and arbitrage, this is exactly what was going on when I was processing Bill's $100K balance transfer. I knew it was savvy, but I didn't understand the benefits it provided. Here are 3 of the benefits (look familiar?)

1) Safety
2) Leverage (MBNA's Money)
3) Guaranteed Growth (1-year CD)

Now, what if Bill knew about IBC on top of the credit card to a 1-year CD strategy?

How much more financially efficient could he have been with a transaction?

Using Imagination and IBC to Enhance Financial Efficiency

Here are 3 options Bill could have used if he had an IBC policy when he was using MBNA's money to create an arbitrage opportunity.

Option 1

Bill had 3 years in a row in which he earned $5K from the credit card to 1-year CD strategy. Bill sent the $5K to his PUA Rider each time he cashed out the 1-year CD. This gave Bill $15K of money he earned from OPM that will increase at 4% guaranteed uninterrupted growth until the day he dies.

Option 2

Bill decided that a 1-year CD making 5% was a nice return but it stopped earning after a year. So, he took the $100K and opened a single premium IBC policy funding the PUA rider for $90K. He knew this would be a long-term play. He also knew that after 40 years, the $90K would grow to $410,487.26 (4% guaranteed uninterrupted growth).

Option 3

Bill decided he wanted to build a rental property portfolio. He knew he needed about $75K to add 3 cash flowing properties. Bill wanted long term cash flow, appreciation and guaranteed growth. Bill had the $75K in cash for the purchase of the 3 cash flowing properties but decided to supercharge his financial efficiency. He took the $100K from MBNA and sent it to his PUA Rider. He then leveraged (loan) his IBC policy for the

$75K needed and added 3 cash flowing properties. He used the $75K cash to qualify for the cash flowing properties and after the mortgages closed, he sent the $75K to his IBC policy to pay the loan. Bill used the extra cash flow from the rental properties to pay the credit card throughout the year and after his 0% term was up on his credit card, he leveraged (loan) his IBC policy to pay off the credit card.

All 3 options have their own merit and you are only limited by your own imagination. I want to break down option 3 to unpack all the moving pieces.

Let's go over what Bill had.

1) Bill had $75K in cash
2) Bill had $100K at 0% for 15 months to use as he wanted
3) Bill had an IBC policy that allowed him to send $100K to his PUA rider

Bill ended up with

1) 3 cash flowing rental properties
2) $90K earning 4% guaranteed uninterrupted growth until the day he dies that was funded by OPM (credit card)
3) Credit card paid back by cash flow from the rental properties and IBC policy leverage (loan)
4) IBC policy loan paid back with $75K cash Bill had
5) Tenants paying mortgages on 3 rental properties

To summarize, Bill used leverage very efficiently, he used financial vehicles he controlled to maximize financial efficiency and he used a limited-time opportunity to build generational wealth. I can't stress enough how much control is interwoven throughout this option and how important it is to be in control of your money. It is the difference between getting by and thriving.

Investor and Business Opportunities

There are some investors and business models that fit very well with an IBC practice.

I will list some out here.

1) Real Estate Investor (especially the fix and flipper)
2) Business Owners with Quarterly Tax Obligations
3) Money Lenders (especially those lending at 6-18 month terms)
4) Business Owners with Seasonal Cash Flow Swings
5) Any Business Involving Flipping Assets

These are just some of models that work well with an IBC practice; there are most certainly more out there.

Read this section a couple of times. Think about how you could apply it to your own unique situation. Allow your creativity and imagination to guide you and write it down. Go over what you have written down and critique it very hard.

Ask yourself, is this the most financially efficient way to do this?

Keep asking the question above every time you are making decisions involving money.

In chapter 6, we will go into one of my favorite topics and one that all money lenders will want to go through and compare to their business models. But before we do that let's talk about the Government.

5
Alternate Funding Sources

There is one other area I want to address when you start looking for money to fund an IBC policy. It is controversial and will get a lot of financial advisors upset, but this is about us, not them.

Government-Sponsored Plans

Do you have any of the following:

1) 401K
2) 403B
3) 457B
4) IRA

If you do, then you have some money to fund an IBC policy. But Ed, my financial advisor, said this is a bad idea. It is a bad idea for them. Now for you, let me ask you to list out the benefits from chapter 3 and run these government plans through them.

Take a deep breath and remember we all have had our money mindsets conditioned to believe a few things that are half-truths at best.

1) You Need Retirement Savings
2) Look at the Average Rate of Return
3) Trust Us We're the Government
4) Deferring Taxes

Let's unpack all these and expose the truth.

You Need Retirement Savings

Is investing the same as saving?

It is most certainly not. If you are saving money, that had better fit the definition of safety (your money has no risk of loss). How do you think folks felt about their retirement savings accounts in 2008? They are not savings accounts; this is gambling with your money to reach an unknown number you need for retirement.

Sure, you can stuff all the money you have in one of these government plans into a money market fund but is that even good?

Do you have full control over your government-sponsored plan?

We don't and worse yet, they can change the rules on us (Secure Act of 2020).

Look at The Average Rate of Return

We beat this marketing gimmick up pretty good in "The Noise Section" in chapter 2. Reread that section if you need to know why mutual fund managers use it to promote their funds.

Trust Us We're The Government

Where do we begin with these jokers?

Go to: usdebtclock.org

Pretty scary stuff. As of the writing of this book, Uncle Sam has racked up $23.2 trillion dollars of debt. These are the same guys who killed pensions, raided social security and created all these government retirement plans.

Do you really think they are going to set up the most efficient financial vehicle you should be putting your money into?

Did you ever think why does the Government care so much about what the stock market is doing?

You would care if you had a $23 trillion dollar bill and your best untapped source of revenue is in your citizen's government-sponsored retirement plans.

Think about it.

Who has control?

You or them?

Deferring Taxes

Are taxes going up or down?

Check out usdebtclock.org one more time before you answer.

I have a deal for you. I will let you invest in the stock market and not pay taxes on your gains and when you do pay, it will be on the total amount of your retirement account. I also can't tell you what the tax rate will be, and I will tell you when you must take it out. Also, if you do access it too early, you owe me 10%. Oh yeah and since I regulate the financial industry, I will know when the most amount of retirement money will have to come out, so don't be surprised if I raise taxes then. You ready to sign up, here is a pen.

Pay your bills when they are due and do business with financially sound individuals and businesses, not those drowning in debt.

How Do I Access The Money?

Take a loan out of your government-sponsored retirement plan if you are able. Use that money to fund an IBC policy and take control back. This will vary from custodian to custodian but investigate it. No one should be punished with onerous ever-changing rules on accessing their money.

What About The Roth 401K/IRA?

It is better than tax-deferred but fails badly if you run the benefits test against it.

What About Self-Directed IRAs?

I have a self-directed Roth IRA and it is the best of the worst of the Government plans. It gives you more control over what you invest in, but there are limitations on how much you can put in. You also risk the Government changing the rules. They have a history of doing that. I'm currently not adding more to my Roth IRA.

I am using the money in it to do real estate lending. But I have a plan of what to do with it on my 59 ½ birthday. Close it out and dump all the cash into my IBC policies. Now I have total control and the Government will not change the rules on existing private contracts in a life insurance policy.

6
The Velocity of Money

My own personal definition of Velocity of Money is:

"How fast your money comes in and goes back out to increase upon itself."

If money is not flowing it is not growing. There are few businesses out there better than the business of lending money for an interest rate. This is where you often hear the phrase "Everyone wants to be the Bank." Banks are very efficient at turning money quickly. Our focus here will be how can you do what banks do, more efficiently and for your own benefit.

Less than a year ago, I set out on a mission to figure out how I could lend money on a small scale and do it using an efficient velocity of money model.

I thought about this for a long time before putting this in the book, but the business I am going to give free publicity to has such an efficient model I can't leave it out. Anyone reading this book can implement this today and for as little as $10. If there is any drawback, it would be that by using this strategy, you don't have the full control of an owner.

The Little Investor's Velocity of Money Champion

I came across Groundfloor in April of 2019 and was instantly intrigued by their model. They are a REG A+ real estate lending marketplace that came about in 2013 when the Jobs Act became law in 2012. They are a real estate crowdfunding platform. There are many real estate crowdfunding platforms out there, but there is only one I know of that provides investors with the following opportunities that fit an efficient velocity of money model.

Groundfloor's Benefits

1) Allows investment into a loan for 1 property
2) Allows a minimum investment as small as $10
3) All loans range from 6 to 12 months in term
4) Reinvestment is very simple
5) 30+ loans always available for funding
6) Groundfloor prefunds all loans before offering them to investors
7) An investor earns the full stated loan interest rate (Groundlfoor makes money on points)
8) Qualified by the SEC

After using the platform for a few months, I stumbled across what shifted my money mindset to recognize the most efficient way to use Groundfloor for velocity of money.

Groundfloor has loans that pay monthly interest or deferred interest. I immediately recognized that investing in loans that paid monthly interest would allow me to lend that money right back out when the interest payments came in. I thought wow that is huge. I then discovered you can do this on less than $10.

Let me elaborate. If you are a Groundfloor investor and you only have a few hundred or thousand dollars lent out, you will only see a minimal amount of interest payments coming in each month. Initially I thought I had to wait until it built up to $10 to lend it out. Not SO!

How excited do we get when we discover a way to increase financial efficiency?

Very

Velocity of Money On $4.33

$4.33 was the exact amount of interest payments that came into my Groundfloor account, when I discovered how to lend it right back out. I went to the deposit money section of my Groundfloor account and put in $5.67 and hit enter. It went through. Wow I thought this just upped the financial efficiency of my money in my Groundfloor account.

Now this may seem like a small amount or not a big deal but, let me assure you that if you can improve the efficient use of the velocity of money model, your money grows much quicker. I now could lend out all the interest payments that came in every month, right back out into new monthly paying loans. Game changer. I don't doubt others have figured this out, but I wanted to share it and give credit to Brian Dally and the team at Groundfloor for offering the little guys a platform to get into real estate investing and utilize the velocity of money concept efficiently.

Velocity of Money and IBC

Remember the term arbitrage from the previous chapter and how it can significantly improve our financial efficiency when applied correctly. Spread investing is the mechanics of arbitrage. Here is an example:

Cost of Capital: 5%
Investment Gain: 10%
Spread: 5%

There is always a cost to capital. There is no free money, someone is always paying for the cost of capital. Many pay it and don't even realize they are paying it (ex- 0% on new car purchases).

Leveraging (loan) an IBC policy, to lend money out at an interest rate more favorable then the cost of capital, is a very efficient model, if you maintain control. Let me take you through an example.

Fix and Flip Example

Ted has an IBC policy with $200K of cash value available. His friend Tony approaches him about a real estate deal he wants to fund. Tony has a property under contract for $100K that requires about $20K worth of work to sell it. The ARV (after repair value) is $200K. Tony asks Ted to loan him $120K to acquire the property and pay his crew to prepare the house for sale.

Ted does his due diligence and verifies that similar houses are selling in 2-4 months for right around $200K. Ted agrees to lend Tony the money.

Here are the terms on Tony's loan from Ted:

Loan: $120K (60% LTV – loan to value)
Interest Rate: 12%
Term Length: 12 months
Points: 2 ($2400)

Ted leverages (loan) his IBC policy for the $120K needed to fund Tony's deal.

Here are Ted's IBC loan terms:

Loan: $120K
Interest Rate: 5% (simple interest of $6K applied)

The Fix and Flip Results

Tony was able to fix the house and sell it in 6 months. He sold it for full ask ($200K).

Here are Tony's final numbers:

Sale Price: $200K
Agent Commission: $5K
Loan Costs: $129,600.00 ($120K (loan) + $2400 (points) + $7200 (interest)
Gross Profit (Subject to Tax): $65,400.00

Ted received $2400 from Tony at the time purchase for the points on the loan. The interest was deferred so at the closing table Ted received $127,200.00.

Here are Ted's final numbers:

Total loan proceeds: $129,600.00
Total IBC loan cost: $123K ($3K of interest charge was credited back to Ted)
Total Profit: $6600.00

Now is there something else working in Ted's favor?

Yes! We did not factor in the fact that Ted's $120K loan was only leveraging his cash value. His $120K never left his cash value and was still earning 4% guaranteed uninterrupted growth, while it was leveraged (loaned) out to Tony. How does that look.

Here are the numbers:

Ted's $120K 4% Earnings for 6 Months: $2400

Now when we look at what really happened for Ted, we can see he paid $600 to make $6600.

But did he even pay the $600 when we think about it?

He did not. Tony paid it for him out of the interest he owed Ted for the loan. Ted paid nothing to his policy loan because he enjoys the benefit of flexibility his IBC policy provides for him. He paid the policy loan off when Tony paid him at the closing table.

Now it is not all rainbows and unicorns for Ted. Ted must pay taxes on the points and interest he earned from Tony.

But again, did Ted really pay the taxes or did Tony pay them at the closing table?

Tony paid them. Ted, if he is a master of the IBC practice, will take what he will owe in taxes and put it into the PUA rider of his IBC policy where it will earn 4% guaranteed uninterrupted growth while waiting to pay the IRS.

Think about this deal. It was a good deal for Tony, who made more money than Ted. But Ted made money by applying financial efficiency at every turn and with little risk or cash out of his own pocket.

Final Thoughts

The velocity of money model works very well with any type of money lending on short-term loans (6-18 months). The more control you have of the vehicle your using to velocitize your money the better. If you can control both sides of the deal that is winning inside your IBC policy and outside in your business.

Did you think of that during the fix and flip example?

What if there was no Tony?

What if Ted lent himself the money for the deal?

If that happened it turns the whole cost of capital idea on its head. If you own the structure (IBC policy) providing the capital and you profit from the deal, then you win twice.

If you have not figured it out yet having an IBC policy to leverage, lowers your cost of capital. Even some of the interest you must pay the insurance company on the policy loan flows back to the owners (IBC policy owners) of the insurance company.

In the next chapter, we will go over company selection and finding an insurance agent.

7
Moving Forward: Selecting an Agent and Insurance Company

When people first hear about IBC they typically take to Google and begin researching. This will lead you down all sorts of rabbit holes and similar-sounding terms to IBC. Many of them will have word plays off the bank, banking, yourself, becoming and the list goes on. Some will say use a HELOC (Home Equity Line of Credit) and others will say use a credit card with your HELOC. The important thing to remember is that IBC is a concept and not a product. As we have established earlier in the book, the most efficient financial vehicle for practicing IBC is dividend paying whole life insurance through a mutual insurance company.

You can lay out the benefits side by side from chapter 3 and run them on any financial vehicle you want to prove it to yourself. Please contact me immediately if you find a different financial vehicle because I want to know. The goal is financial efficiency not buying life insurance. It is the money mindset at play. I'm not locked into life insurance if someone finds a better way and neither should you.

Selecting an Insurance Agent

Before we get too deep into this, I want to share what I almost did but trusted my inner guidance to say NO to. I almost set up a universal index insurance policy with a stockholder beholden life insurance company. It was sold to me as sure you can practice IBC with it. Long story short, this would have been a mistake and in no way would have benefited future generations of my family. If someone tries to sell you on any other type of life insurance product other than one mentioned in the first paragraph of this section, you can be sure they are trying to jump on the IBC bandwagon to push their products and agenda.

I highly suggest you go straight to the source (Nelson Nash Institute) and find an authorized practitioner. You can find one at:

infinitebanking.org/finder

Anyone listed on this finder list has been through training in IBC and certified by the Nelson Nash Institute. You can use other life insurance agents, just make sure they fully understand IBC and you do as well.

Your Conversations with An Agent

Starting an IBC policy is not a watch a couple videos, read some blog posts or a book and you're ready to go. Educate yourself and be ready for multiple calls. Ask questions and go through every scenario you need to make an educated decision. A big part of that education will come from the back and forth with the agent. If that is not going on or there is reluctance on the agent's part to have in-depth conversations, then move on to the next one. This is about you and your family's financial future and not to be taken lightly. The comfort level you have with your agent and the knowledge sharing back and forth is key. This is a long-term relationship you're forming and a long-term financial commitment. In the resource section at the end of the book, I will list some folks I have dealt directly with and others who have a good understanding of IBC.

Which Mutual Life Insurance Company?

This, believe it or not, is a highly debated topic among some of the IBC agent practitioners. There are some that push the big 4 (Mass Mutual, New York Life, Guardian and Northwestern Mutual). Others believe the concept itself is more important than focusing on who the mutual insurance carrier should be. I personally have 1 policy with one of the big 4 and one with another mutual life insurance company.

The big 4 have a proven financial track record, while some of the other smaller ones are slightly behind them. In the end, it comes down to you and what works for you. I can tell you there are a few things I like about the IBC policy I have set up with the smaller company more than I do with the one I have with the big company.

There is also the long game at play. Once you start using an IBC policy and you see the benefits show up in your financial life, you will want more than one policy. My family has 3 and that number will only increase as our practice matures and opportunities present themselves.

8
Questions You May Have

When you first learn about IBC it can be overwhelming and you will have doubts, fears and questions, lots of questions. As I have stressed throughout the book, the biggest obstacle you will face is your money mindset. Keep an open and curious mind, educate yourself and ask questions. I will take you through common questions that will come up, to assist you on your journey in learning and understanding IBC.

Questions

1) What if I can't make the premium payments?

There are usually 4 payment options available to you. They are monthly, quarterly, semi-annually and yearly. I made the mistake back in 2015 of focusing on the overall premium I would have to pay and therefore lost years of compounding due to indecision. Here are the numbers I was facing and how they play into the question.

My First IBC Policy

Overall Premium: $8K
Base Premium: $2K
PUA Rider: $6K

My hang-up was what if I can't pay $8K a year. The PUA Rider is not required to keep the policy in force. The financial obligation required on the numbers above is $2K. My money mindset was not prepared to commit to $8K a year. Had my agent and I discussed this in detail, I might have been able to get past it. I did not ask, and he didn't bring it up. The assumption was made that I was not ready. I own that completely. Always ask questions was my takeaway and my advice to you.

2) What happens if I can't make the whole PUA Rider premium payment?

Piggybacking on the previous section, we now know that payments (think of them as deposits) into the PUA Rider are not required. It is perfectly acceptable to only send $2K to your PUA Rider for a given year. In 1988 the MEC (Modified Endowment Contract) came into existence.

This restriction was put into place to stop small death benefit life insurance policies with very large cash sides, from being set up to avoid taxes. A 7 year pay test is what the IRS came up with, to make sure that the example below never happens again.

You Just MEC'd Your Policy

Overall Premium: $5 Million
Base Premium: $5K
PUA Rider: $4.995 Million

Now all whole life insurance contracts are limited to 3-9 times the base premium that can be put into the PUA Rider. The MEC 7 year pay test allows for carryover from year to year regarding the PUA Rider.

Here is how it would adjust based on paying $2K to the PUA Rider in year 2 of an IBC policy:

PUA Rider Scenario 1

Year 1: Full $8K paid

Year 2: $2K Base Premium paid and $2K of the available $6K PUA Rider paid

Year 3: PUA Rider has carryover of $4K from year 2 and a total of $10K can be sent to the PUA Rider.

This can go on up to year 7. If you run into a couple of tight years financially, each year will carry over to the next, regarding the PUA Rider allowable funding amount.

Here is the previous scenario with the MEC considerations included:

PUA Rider Scenario 1

Year 1: Full $8K paid

Year 2: $2K Base Premium Paid and $2K of the available $6K PUA Rider Paid

Years 3 and 4: Nothing has been sent to the PUA Rider.

Year 5: PUA Rider has carryover of $4K (year 2) + $6K (year 3) + $6K (year 4)

How much can you send to the PUA Rider in year 5? $16K

Most of us have been through a tough year or two financially. The flexibility of an IBC policy, addresses this and provides us with options when funding the PUA Rider.

3) I don't understand what 3 to 9 times the base premium is and why I may need a term insurance rider?

The Government (IRS) is good at setting regulations but not in seeing the loopholes they create with their regulations. The MEC test is all about the death benefit amount in relation to the cash, that can go into an insurance policy. There are other factors, but they are based on an individual's age, etc. They matter little in answering this question.

Here is an example with rough numbers:

IBC Policy (3 times the base premium) (No term insurance rider)

Overall Premium: $8K
Base Premium: $2K
PUA Rider: $6K

IBC Policy (9 times the base premium) (term insurance rider included)

Overall Premium: $35K
Base Premium: $3.5K
PUA Rider: $31.5K
Term Insurance Rider: $500

The setup of an IBC policy with 9 times the base premium must have a 1-year renewable term insurance rider attached to it. Without a term insurance rider (sometimes called blended insurance) you can only fund 3 times the base premium. This is a creative way of getting more cash into your IBC policy. These types of IBC policies typically have 9 times the base premium funding periods anywhere from 1 to 15 years. In year 16, the 1-year term rider drops and your max PUA Rider funding drops to 3 times the base premium. The cost of the 1-year term insurance rider is paid out of your cash within the PUA Rider. So, if you decide on an IBC policy using this strategy, you will see the required premium to keep your policy in force will now include the cost of the base premium and $500 or so dollars (PUA Rider). The reason for this is the 1-year term rider must be paid for. Take that into account when understanding your required overall premium payment. You also may encounter some insurance companies that have the blended (term) insurance rider for a small amount as part of the 3 to 1. It can be company practice dependent.

Insurance Agent Thoughts (The 3 to 9)

I want to make you aware that agents have varying opinions on policy design when it comes to the 3 to 9 range. Don't be swayed one way or the other, on what you end up choosing based on one agent's opinion. The decision is based on your financial goals, current financial situation and comfort level. I have both a 3 and a 9 IBC policy. Both fit into my financial strategy and I am comfortable with them. Ask candid questions and get in the weeds.

4) Why is an IBC more efficient the longer it is in force?

The first couple of years, you will be paying for the cost of insurance (death benefit). This is not free and most who rip the rate of return on a whole life insurance policy, ignore the cost of the death benefit. It is not free! Ask the agent you're working with to go over how the dividend works with the base premium. Almost all policies have very little in the way of dividends in relation to the premium you are paying to the base (death benefit). As the years go by, the dividend the base premium is earning gets larger and larger. It is a long-term tailwind you will see make a big impact after 10 years or so.

Think of the cash value as your short-term bank to utilize. In the early years, this will be built up by your PUA Rider deposits. The base premium is your long-term bank. It earns small dividends that go into your cash value (provided you set them to buy additional paid-up insurance). Once they hit your cash value, they now become a part of the cash value that earns 4% guaranteed uninterrupted growth. Once your base premium is earning dividends equal to what you are required to pay each year, to keep your policy in force, you now have an IBC policy that can fund itself, if necessary. The power of that is often overlooked by short-sighted critics. I'm going to end this section and this question with a quote I am tweaking to apply to IBC, from Earl Nightingale.

"Don't let the fear of contributing large premiums to your IBC policy stand in the way of your doing it. The time will pass anyway, we might just as well let our IBC policies do the very best, they possibly can."

9
The Bigger Picture and Final Thoughts

In the United States, we have many things that are out of our control. In 1913, income taxes became permanent and the Federal Reserve was created. In 1971, the dollar was removed from being pegged to gold. We are all aware of how infrequently the Government changes something that is already in place. Think about the IRS, the Federal Reserve, Social Security and Medicare being completely shut down.

What do you think the odds are of any of those Government institutions completely vanishing?

I'm not pointing any of this out to be political but rather to lay out the facts and the odds. As you are aware, if you visited usdebtclock.org, the country is in massive debt. The numbers are so large it can seem mind-boggling.

How will we pay for it?

Do you believe Government is the answer?

I say you are the answer and I am the answer.

We all have a choice to recognize our commonalities as human beings and change. Not forced top down (Government) change but an individual deciding to change because they can control that. We see it all the time in our society. We are not inspired by Congress or a local government. We are inspired by Gandhi, Mother Teresa, Martin Luther King. It is the individual who inspires us. I would not be writing this book without Nelson Nash turning inward, looking for an answer and finding IBC. He inspired me to take action in my life and to give, by sharing through this book.

As Nelson Nash has said, "It starts at the you and me level." All the problems and solutions to anything in life start with one person, with an idea, who shares it with a friend. Keep that in mind as many folks struggle with health, finances and growing political indifference. All change starts with one person and an idea. But the real meaningful, lasting change comes from the bottom up, not top down. We can all start by embracing IBC and changing the flow of money to us not away from us. One person at a time committing to make a change. The more of us who control our money, the better chance, we have to save our future.

Final Thoughts

We have covered a lot of ground in this book and I want to end it with personal observations on money, life and the search for peace, fulfillment and a better life for ourselves and our families.

I believe that we all have a common thread among us as human beings, to experience peace (contentment) in our lives. Money alone is not the answer. It is a piece of the overall puzzle but alone it leads to an empty life. I have stressed the money mindset throughout the book because it is the key to a healthy relationship with money. Be very careful with how your money mindset ties into your religious and spiritual beliefs. Explore it, be curious and open to change. I encourage you to turn inward and find your way. I offer you the statement below. Find your place in it, that works for you and use it as a base to live your best life.

"Imagine all your needs are taken care of from a financial perspective. You have the freedom to explore, imagine and create. What would that look like to you? What beautiful experiences can you see for you and your family. Imagine the peacefulness and fulfillment of living your passions every day. There is nothing holding you back, everything is

Resources

Books

1) Becoming Your Own Banker by Nelson Nash
2) Building Your Warehouse of Wealth by Nelson Nash
3) How Privatized Banking Really Works by Carlos Lara and Robert P Murphy
4) The AND Asset by Caleb Guilliams

There are other books, but I have read the above multiple times and the first 3 are must-reads in understanding IBC. The reason I listed Caleb Guilliam's book is because it is short, to the point and conveys the benefits very well. He also is young, has an inspiring mission of financial independence through IBC and an individual's unique ability, that will be critical in carrying the IBC message to the younger generation.

Podcasts

1) Banking With Life Podcast
2) The Lara-Murphy Show
3) The Banking Breakdown
4) Better Wealth Podcast
5) Wealth Without Wall Street Podcast
6) The Infinite Wealth Podcast
7) Wealth Talks Podcast
8) Real Estate Money School
9) The Insurance Pro Blog Podcast
10) The Money Advantage Podcast
11) Dollars and Nonsense

YouTube

I will only talk about one channel here. If you are looking for the most in-depth analysis of illustrations, companies, side by side comparisons and getting into the weeds with examples, then check out IBC Global Inc's channel.

Full disclosure I have policies with them.

Steve Parisi provides an immense amount of great content that will help anyone interested in IBC become more knowledgeable. FYI he is an authorized practitioner.

Video

1) Nelson Nash's Seminar on DVD
2) Banking With Life DVD
3) This is Nelson Nash

Blog

1) Ryan Griggs on Medium – Ryan is a phenomenal writer and conveys IBC as well as anyone I have ever read.

Austrian Economics

IBC fits well into the school of Austrian Economics. If you love to read, go down the rabbit hole and explore Menger, Mises, Hayek, Rothbard, Hazlitt and anyone tied to the Mises Institute or FEE. It will only enhance the foundation on understanding why IBC works very well.

Made in the USA
Monee, IL
04 November 2026

67378640R10046